The years we have [...]
mean so much to me as
our bond grows and grows
Thank you and I love you.

Hark E. Lanier
Pappa
10/20/12

Between

Harold E. Lannom

Order this book online at www.trafford.com
or email orders@trafford.com

Most Trafford titles are also available at major online book retailers.

Printed in the United States of America.

ISBN: 978-1-4669-6129-6 (sc)
ISBN: 978-1-4669-6128-9 (hc)
ISBN: 978-1-4669-6130-2 (e)

Library of Congress Control Number: 2012918178

Trafford rev. 09/28/2012

 www.trafford.com

North America & international
toll-free: 1 888 232 4444 (USA & Canada)
phone: 250 383 6864 ♦ fax: 812 355 4082

Dedication

For Adrienne
1934-2012

Acknowledgements

I would like to especially recognize;
Lo Caudle, for the years spent reading and sharing
Pam Leonard, for believing in me and hours of reading
Joyce Watts, for life long friendship and encouragement
Shelley Wilson, first my student now my teacher
I love you all,

                      Harold

ROMAN NUMERAL ONE

Between

I want to live in the between
Where there is movement
Where the unknown rules

Between
  Earth and sky
    Morning and evening
     Sunshine and shadow
Between
  Sleeping and waking
    Up and down
     Left and right
Between
  Father and son
    Man and woman
     Birth and death
Between
  Planting and harvest
    Seen and unseen
     Love and hate

I want to live in the between
Where the unexpected and unknown
Flow easily as a meandering river
Between the know-alls and know-nothings

Enchanted Garden

Hush! Don't tell.
There are fairies in your garden.
Little people are shy,
Yet I heard them in the trees
And I saw them dance
On the water as it falls.

Some find their way
Into your house
When you are all alone
To dance a merry jig
And sing a bawdy song.

You may not know
That they are there,
But when you sing and dance
Look around and see them
Dancing on the stairs.

They love to play tricks
And when you are not looking
Take a trinket or treasure
To enjoy at their leisure
At their home in the grotto.

You can not see them
Unless they choose
To take a mortal form,
Yet you will know they are there
When they tangle up your hair

The little ones have blest you
I can tell it by your laughter
And the sweetness of your song.
They are present in the love you share
With all who come along.

Mist

Above this elemental earth

a spirit
a mist
a cloud

pure air
flowing
over all

creating
color and
softness

gray stone
turned to
crystals

brown earth
turned to
emerald

mist spirit
penetrate
my flesh

with visions
music
smiles

Winter's Hold

Trees keep a lively rhythm outside my window,
as March tries to hurry the arrival of spring.
Winter does not surrender easily as
frost on roofs keep me aware.

Yet I watch for signs of what is to come,
the plum tree's pink coat,
the pussy willow buds,
the yellow green of alder leaves.

The movement of tree branches
and the water filled sky
do not give me any encouragement

Snowberries

Winter in her dark coat
of leafless sticks
woven together with fir,
pine, balsam and
clinging moss,
surprises the eye with
round buttons of
pure white
drops of snow,
even here
where there is
none.

Morning

It is freezing this morning
before dawn and
the moon is a snowball
against the black sky.

The nocturnals are returning
to dens and nests
to get warm again,
while we of the day
welcome this last moment
of quiet before the rattle
of pans and dishes
breaks the quiet
as we prepare
to break the fast.

This short treasured moment
fills me with peace and hope.

Ground-hog Day

One fleeting moment
wrapped in the
wool of winter

we stand
observing the
ritual of divination

where winter hangs
on the thread
of a shadow.

But look around
my fellow frozen,
can you not see

you also cast
a shadow.
The sun is still alive

and slowly
will return to
warm the earth.

The hog says
winter is not over
but the sun is returning.

The frozen buds
begin to swell with
golden nectar and

the scent of
early spring
to gladden the heart.

So now
within me
stirs a smile,

a laugh,
a desire to
come out and play.

Thanks For The Rain

Thanks for the rain.
The delivery system
Could use a little work.
Thunder was OK but,
The lightening
Over the top.

Next time in summer
When clouds pile up
Like the foam on my pint,
Just drop the wet stuff.
Leave out the theatrics.

While we're at it,
One hundred degrees
Is more than just hot.
When you used mud on
The sixth day, you didn't
Use any asbestos.

Out side of that,
The strawberries were good
And we really liked the peaches.
You could hold back a little
On the zucchini
But, thanks for the rain.

Autumn

Out of the humus of the dark earth
Rises a stench of decaying life
Untended poorly nourished
Under the sheltering firs

Now as days become shorter
And the sun hides behind clouds
The first rain arrives to release
A dormant mushroom
Continuing the cycle of life

Autumn lessons are dark and subtle
While spring sings in high pitch
Altos proclaim the glory of fall
The tempo slows and volume is low
For contrast there is thunder and lightning
And a small mushroom message

Water Mother

On my annual visit to the shore

Wrapped in my own smallness
I see the stalwart rocks
The crashing waves
   Wind driven
   Spray tipped

Life creating water
From your womb we came
Pushed on the land by your
Life giving surge

Though the struggle has been hard
Comfort and strength you still provide
Sloshing water from shore to shore
Reforming the land

Today you are dressed well with
White lace fringe on the
Hem of your dark garment
Adorned by cormorants
While gulls bow at your feet

Siuslaw

It is Sunday and sitting by the window
watching the river flowing out to sea
the day's entertainment appears
gulls gracefully landing on narrow pilings
graceful in flight gentle in landing
ducks diving their buffleheads
deep in search of food
while the kingfisher wags his head
looking for the unsuspecting fish.

My eyes are drawn upward
to the dunes on the other side
rising straight from the water's edge
in smooth flowing lines
big rolling hills of sand
ocean delivered
transported by the winds of summer
occasional outcropping of rock
and in the distance a few trees survive

Monday and the actors have not returned
to encore their Sunday performance
was it just for me they danced upon the water
and pirouetted on the pilings
maybe they don't perform on Mondays
reserving their best for Sunday or
perhaps they have moved on to
another venue their manager has arranged.

Fred

Out the front door down the steps
to get the morning paper
greeted by cawcawcawcaw
      (good morning)
I respond, "Good morning to you too Fred,"
(our name for him)

Hopping down another branch
from up on the very top
where Fred likes to sit,
I ask, "How was your night?"

kkkkkkkkkkkkkkkkkkkkkkkk
  *(The kids kept me up pushing and shoving.
    I had to go sit in anther tree.")*
Hopping down another branch or two
"Fred I am sorry, and today could you
not sit on the branch over my car"
cawcacaca   *(ha, ha, ha)*

Coming closer he lands lightly on the ground.
I ask, "What is it like to be a crow?"
Caw   (*what*)
Jumps up to a low branch
then up one or two more.
Caw   (*what*)

I guess Fred is not a philosophical crow.
From up in the higher branches comes the
kkkkkkkkkkkkkkkkkkkkkkkkkkkkkkkkkk
(*I've been trying to tell you,*
I am not a crow,   I am a raven)
caw caw ca ca kkkkkkkkkkkkkk
(*ha ha ha, and you can quoth me on that.*)

A Sisters' Morning

The dark cloud heavy with water
drops itself slowly over the mountaintop
lowering into the valleys

spilling its contents on peaks
and clear blue water of
lakes and rivers below.

A rainbow begins to form
then fades before its work is done
leaving imagination to fill in colors.

The rising sun
lands on the pasture
turning it to gold.

I have found the end of the rainbow.
I look again and it is gone,
a field of green remains.

Sunrise Facing West

I get up in the dark and find my way to the kitchen.
When the coffee is finished and
the paper retrieved from the porch,
cup in hand, I climb the stairs to my room, where
I will read,
       pray, and
             meditate.
I reach out to bless the day, then close my eyes.

When I open them again, I am startled by the light.
The sun has risen above the horizon
and the light from the risen sun
has broken through in brilliant gold.

Is it I only who hears the
Trumpet blast and
       The cymbal crash accompanied
            By the whole company of brass.

I am not alone for
The welcoming trees reach higher
       And sway with the music
           Dancing in the warm breeze.

Brighter and brighter
The landscape appears
As the gold intensifies and the music swells.
I am present at the opening day of creation.

Late Summer

I guess you could call this late summer
It isn't fall for weeks yet
The flowers that have survived
Are of a darker hue

The pinks, soft yellows, light blues,
Have gone now replaced by
Golden yellow, burnt orange,
Flaming red, and deep purple

The sweet peas replaced by trumpet vines
Pale poppies by splendid sunflowers
Delicate delphiniums by flaming asters.

The days are shorter and the nights colder
Yet the days are hot when the sun
Burns through the early morning fog

This is a between season
Often overlooked as we
Remember summer days or
Anticipate the more spectacular autumn

The betweens of life are hard to see
Overshadowed by spectacular events

ROMAN NUMERAL TWO

On the Day I Was Born

On the day I was born
God was on vacation
Possibly Prince Edward Island
Enjoying a church supper
That magnificent tradition
Of lobster and mussels
With lots of butter
And strawberry shortcake
For heaveners vacation there

A guardian angel ushered me into this life
Unfortunately he drinks at times
But he loves music and people
He must have had a few that night
He took me to the wrong house
They were not expecting an arrival

Someday he and I will
Vacation on the island
And eat lobster and mussels
With lots of butter
And strawberry shortcake

Presence

mysterious mystical
reality beyond flesh
being unbound
by time or place
entering soul like
into experience
changing lives
for those
who know,
leave us not alone

Faces

With the first rays of sunlight
my heart cries out to thee,
creator of the moon and stars,
let me see thee in all I meet.

At the nadir of the sun's course
let not my thirst for mercies
distract from the chance to see
thy face in all I meet.

When day is done, my work complete,
may I not in my tiredness fail
to thank thee for all the faces
that gave me a vision of thee.

Affirmations

An ordinary day
The sun was late
The air was cool
September is here

A neighbor says,
"I missed you at the market"
A rise in the corner of my mouth
Says "thank you"

An old friend writes
"I thought of you today
Hope all is well"
My moist eyes soften

Affirmations of caring
In and ordinary day
Turn my thoughts
To sunlight

A granddaughter's
"I love you, papa"
Is the noontime
Of this ordinary day.

Waiting

Into the dark night
No moon or stars
Clouds hanging low
And a cold north wind

A light flickers
As a fire burns
Where shepherds
Are trying to stay warm

On the hillside
In the valley
The darkness is not
Like any other winter night

Somewhere out there
Comes the word
Comes the baby
Comes the Christ

At midnight
A bell is heard
And then far away
The sound of many bells

Christ is born

Stones In a Pool

The Priest rises to offer prayers for the church, the environment, national leaders, the sick and those who have died, including the men and women killed in Iraq.

the names fall like
stones in a pool of water
stone after stone after stone
each ripple going out
reminds me of a parent, child,
wife, lover, friend
whose cries and tears I hear
and I want to cry out
stop the reading
stop the killing

another name
another stone
another ripple
and I know it will go on
as it has for years without end

Lord, have mercy

Dust

"*Thou art dust,*"
 The priest intones
With blackened thumb
 He marks me
With the ashes
 From the palms we waived
Shouting
 "*Hosanna*"
Hurrah for the new hero
 The new leader
We will follow
 Until your dustness shows

 Remember now our cheers
 For champions
And leaders
 Whose dust we didn't see
Remember now
 The doped athlete
The adulterous politician
 The pedophile priest
Still we look for
 One not made of dust
Whose crown will not
 Tarnish and rust

Remember, oh man
 Thou art dust

Freedom

My country 'tis of thee
>*What is that I hear*

Sweet land of liberty
>*Ten thousand feet shackled by poverty*

Of thee I sing
>*Ten thousand voices crying for food*

Land where our fathers died
>*Fathers seeking searching for work*

Land of the pilgrims pride
>*Mothers feeding their children not themselves*

From every mountain side
>*In every city street*

Let freedom ring

ROMAN NUMERAL THREE

Miscellany

My Muse

My muse has left me
With a blank sheet of paper
A black fine point pen
And the space between is large

My hand is still, waiting instructions
From somewhere somehow somewho
While emptiness between pen and paper
Is full of echoes of things past

Return muse and direct my hand
Touch the pen to the paper and
Give life to the words
That spill with the ink

I wait and in the waiting
Find a voice growing louder
"Your muse is not available
Please leave a message at the tone"

The Safe Place

I tried to write a poem
Of red leaves and gentle rain
Long nights and how
I feel lost in autumn

What I really wanted
Was to tell you who I am
And how it feels
To have you for a friend

But red leaves and gentle rain
Cold nights and warm sun
Make up the framework of our days
And I am safe writing about autumn

You Know What I Think?

You know what I think?
I think that little fairies,
the size of a small gnat,
   very very very small
    (They come in many
     sizes you know)
carry words and pictures,
sounds and symbols,
sometimes even whole sentences.

Finding an unguarded ear,
deposit their gift
and buzzzzzzzz away.
We the unsuspecting recipient exclaim,
"Now where did that come from."

Haiku

A bufflehead duck
swimming up stream dives alone
for breakfast morsels.

The kingfisher sits
waiting for a passing fish
to fill his belly.

Wild red strawberries
with ice cream and blueberries
makes the fourth of July.

New Banks

Where is the Sunlight Savings Bank
Where rays are deposited every year
I would like to make a withdrawal
Perhaps 400 rays scattered throughout
This December day

I wonder if there is a Time Savings and Loan
Funded by the deposits of those
Time saving devices we have at home
Making loans to the many people
Who never seem to have enough

This Is

The rudderless ship of was
rests rusting in the harbor
while in the distance
the siren song of will be
calls to is
whose sails are full and
whose sleek form
plows eagerly on
through swell and spray
for ever and ever

The Card In The Window

How much longer
will there be
someone to remember

the ice man with his
tongs and leather shield
against the cold

stopping at the house
with the card in the window
reading I-C-E

entering the kitchen
putting a 25 block
in the top of the ice box

neighborhood children
following close behind the truck
picking up slivers of ice

for cooling the tongue
on a hot August day
in Riverside County California

They took my Billy

They took my Billy away
to fight in a foreign land,
they did not know he could not fight
with such sweet and tender hands.
They said, "We'll teach him, Ma'am,
of that you can be sure."

They could not know
how much it tore my heart
to see him leave knowing
he will never be the same
of that I could be sure.

His golden hair and
eyes like mountain lakes,
his voice of silver,
a poet's mind not made for war
for death and brutal carnage.

Return he did but
not as I remembered
for now he is a man
and manly things he does enjoy
to swear and drink
and smoke and whore.

For me, my heart is sad
I do not have the boy I had.
The poet is there but
harsh and bitter are his words,
it is a manly thing to do

0200 March 26 1945, near St. Goar Germany, the 89th Infantry Division, 353rd Regiment, 1st Battalion, Company A crossed the Rhine.

Somewhere in the silence	silence
Shuffling feet scrape the earth	silence
Fear rises like a cloud	silence
In the midnight black	black

Wait the command	wait
When will it come	fear
Rise up go now	run

Bursting bombs red flares white flares rifle shots exploding shells run run keep low get in the boats keep low shells explode

One left behind	blood			
Lying on the river bank	silence			
Call for medic gone	wait			
Into the midnight blackness	silence	silence	silen	sil

Echoes In Flint

Standing by
A pillar of
The abbey
At St. Edmonds
I hold
In my hand
A flint
Fallen to the
Ground
It echoes
The sound
Of horses
And I can
Hear men
Shouting
Complaints
Against the
King

A chill runs
Through me
As I stand on
Holy ground
Where men
Brave enough
To challenge a
King
Wrote the
Great
Magna Carta
Tears of gratitude
Streak my cheek
Remembering
Their courage
And wisdom

Meaning

A rock is a rock
is a rock is a rock

except the one
from Bury St. Edmunds
containing echoes
of the Magna Carta

or the volcanic rock
from Mammoth
packed miles
for friendship

or the one
in the desert
we sat on
reading e.e.cummings
and drinking wine.

On Entering Oregon

What did I expect to find,
A paradise where rivers flowed
Mountains rose out of the ocean
Where there was space to grow
A quiet home in a field of huckleberries

I entered this new world starry eyed
My heart full of hope
For fishing everyday
Eating blackberries all summer
A simple life without pretense

Most of what I hoped for I found
Fish, huckleberries, quiet and green
The rest I brought with me
My own complexities and pretenses
The scenery had changed
I had not

Imaging

Imaging a world beyond
    this place and
        it's every-dayness
with chores
    and duties
        and repetitive routines
creating a wonder
    that lifts the spirits
        to sunshine and
            sweet harmonies
The vacuum a private jet to lands I've never seen, shopping in spicy noisy markets in cities that may not exist, wading in a South Sea Island while laundry churns
There are no limits
    Except a return is required
A soft landing is achieved with a glass of wine at 5

Phone Call

What can I offer you
in return for the comfort
and joy you give me
so that in one phone call
a smile appears on my face
and what was a chore, a burden
is now lightened, made easy

Lost Opportunity

The committee sat before me
The judges of my ability
To teach children to sing
Their smile-less faces worry me
I do well with happy people

The thin lipped one requests
"Please sit down at the piano and play"
I do not understand
I want to teach children to sing
Somebody else can teach them to play
"I do not play the piano"
I reply with irritation

"You graduated from a major college
You majored in music
And you do not play the piano"

"I guess that states it very well.
It was not from lack of trying"
I explain with irritation

"If you wanted to be a music teacher
You should have been playing piano at 5"

> *Where has this lady been*
> *Out in the California sun*
> *Did she have a childhood or*
> *Was she hatched full grown*
> *With all those wrinkles in place*

In a shaky voice I finally reply
"Madam when I was 5 I wanted to be a fireman"

I wonder about the children
I could have taught to sing
How many can play the piano

The Backward Look

The fire of long lost passion
Is recalled in grey ash
Where only memories tricks
Can see a spark

The sight of a swelling breast
Once fanned passion into a fire
Now stirs the ashes of remembrance
When settled returns
My spirit to untroubled rest

Age has its benefits
Beyond pensions and Medicare
The backward look is calmer
A vision in soft sepia tones
Where fire once raged

Do Not Go Away

Fear strikes with sharp teeth
Heavy and quickened pulse
Shallow breath cold palms
Muted images of aloneness
Deserted lost excluded

> *I am 9 again*
> *Where there were 2*
> *Now there are 3*
> *Choose me not him*

Fight the acid eating my resolve
Fear wins the battle
Run my mind insists
But where can I run
There are no places to go

> *I will never play with him*
> *Tears rise quickly*
> *Swallow hard*
> *Grit your teeth*
> *The hurt digs in deeper*

Comes now the touch
The voice the presence
Gentle loving kind
Fear abates
The game begins again

> *Hey want to play*
> *You can be first baseman*
> *Fight back resentment*
> *Join the game*
> *I believe it is over*

Years go by the speed of light
Yet not one that doesn't
Repeat the story of pain
The fear of exclusion
Being lost deserted
Alone   alone   alone   alone

Waiting

I waited for you this morning
You did not come
Or were you there
In some disguise

I searched for you
In silence words visions
You did not come
Were you speaking a
Language I do not know

I waited until
I fell asleep
Did you come then
I thought I heard my name

ROMAN NUMERAL FOUR

Counselor

What Can I Give

For many years they have come
One by one or two by two to my
Office door revealing their pain
Their fear their anger

I offer
An ear to hear
A mind to think
A tongue to speak
A life experienced

They seek
A bag of tricks
Soothing conundrums
Rules to live by
All these they have
And do not follow

They need
A broad horizon
An empty canvas
Some locksmith tools
A story or song

I provide assurance
They need not see only
The dirt under their feet
Nor the canvas of their life
Painted by someone else
Nor live within the prison bars
Of guilt and shame
Nor tell the story
Written by others

I give them
A moment of peace
Silence touch
The exposure of my heart

Is it enough
It is all I have

Carpe Diem

The number of days
grow shorter
to see the sun
to be forgiven
and forgive
to love
and be loved
to know the joy
of touching lives
and being touched

The Counselor

I

They sit in silence
Facing each other not looking
Silence broken by unspoken words
They dare not utter
Feelings they can not express

Each darkly into their own thoughts
Thoughts of opportunities lost
Of dreams broken apart by reality
And by words unspoken
Caught on a mobius strip of self protection

II

She enters the office with purpose
A smile and a quick step
Clothes make up hair
All perfectly done

She chooses the straight back chair
With hands folded and ankles crossed
Begins to talk of work family weather

The verbal camouflage
Concealing pain and fear
The eyes behind the makeup
Glisten with poorly held teats

III

Slumped in her chair
A middle aged woman
Eyes half closed
Nervously plays with Kleenex
In barely audible tones
She unveils the darkness
She lives with every day

Her graying hair
Falls over her face
Hiding a new stream of tears
Continues to work the Kleenex
Until she reaches for another

The room seems darker
Despair fills the air

IV

He has done well in business
Is considered successful by many
Married three children
Expensive home and car
With pictures to show

A strong clear voice
Lasts for ten minutes until
A monotonous voice creeps in
And confession begins
Revealing pain no money can fix

Dull vacant eyes
Imagining a future
Which he dreads
Therapy begins

V

Many the secrets I hold in trust
Knowing more than I want
Telling nothing of what I know
Having a vision I can not share

For me the road is long
And the burden gets heavy
I can not lay it down
Only press on
Hearing their pain and fear

Rough Seas

The seas are rough
With *if* and *when*
And the dangerous shoals of
Should and *could*
And the most dangerous
Rocks of *tradition*

A firm hand on the wheel
And a heart that says *this is*

Today

There was
There maybe
This is

ROMAN NUMERAL FIVE

Saints
And
Sinners

A Cauldron of Joy

Your image lively in my mind
Kisses still burning my face
Stirring mind heart and soul

To see you
To hear you
To touch you
A gift
For which I say
"thank you"
And smile

I love the moments
I spend with you
Treasures I store
For the long months
In between

Surrounded by Love

Every morning
I wrap myself in
A quilt of love
Counting the stitches
Imagining the fingers
Denying pain
To complete this gift

Hanging above me
A banner
A heron
Prepared by
Those same hands
Here I read and write

Through out the house
Reminders of love
Quilted hangings
Table runners
Pillow tops

Everywhere I turn
There is loves creation
Manifest in beauty
Given with joy

Norma

Across the table
    you sat
        and listened
while I talked
    of many things
        until

I realized
    you were
        silent

In your presence
    grace
freely given
    in silence
        a holy place

That stillness
    remains
        all else
           gone

Bonded

When first I saw you
> *how many years ago was that*

I had no idea that you would change my life
A head full of plans and ideas
Had no room for you until you smiled
> *A flicker of light I could not ignore*

You offered words gently spoken
with no intent to persuade or change me
until we found ourselves
> *so temporarily*

bonded

On such fleeting moments does life pivot

Martha

It was black and white in a leather frame
But it was the portrait I kept with me
For all the years of absence we experienced.

Alone in the barracks I talked to you and
Always kept you on the shelf next to my cot.
You survived stuffed in a duffle bag and
Arrived home with me safe from the war.

I loved that picture as I loved you
Until I returned and found
You were to marry someone else.

Time helped heal the hurt pride.
The dream would not be silenced until
I found it was your image I loved

Your presence provided a dream,
An incentive to survive.
Thank you Martha of Idaho for the
Image and inspiration you provided a soldier
In the midst of war's confusion.

For John At Eighty

Eighty is a good round number
At which point we try not to be.
When written in numerals "80"
Its roundness is exquisite.

Having achieved this round milestone,
You have already endured the
Indignities of aging, so now
There isn't much else to embarrass you.

Hospital gowns, prostate exams
Colon research, sphincter control,
As for gas, let it rrrrrrripppppp
You have earned the privilege.

Cancel your membership in AARP,
They take in 50 year old kids.
Who needs that indignity?
Subscribe to surfer magazine,
Confuse the mailman and worry your wife.

Talk to everybody you meet.
They won't understand what you are saying,
And they will be afraid to admit it.
That includes talking to yourself.

When the priest comes to call
Lock up your liquor cabinet.
When relatives come to visit
Make a reservation at a motel
For them.

So, my dear friend, John,
After February 9th
Do any friggen thing you want.
You have earned it.

I Saw You

I saw you in the living room window
Waving good bye while holding your baby
I saw you at the kitchen table
Drinking your coffee black with sugar
I saw you in the foggy mirror
As I combed my thinning hair
I saw you crossing the street
With your basket of groceries
I saw you at the neighborhood park
Contentedly reading a book of poems
I saw you in the flashing smile
Of a young girl walking by
I saw you at the noon hour
And again at sunset
I saw you everywhere I looked today
And marveled at how
You have invaded my mind

Silent Canary

What has imprisoned you
Sweet singing bird
Wishes, desires, prying eyes,
Fear, pleasure, choices
So that now as the door is open
You can not fly away

Every day adding color
To someone else's life
Giving comfort where needed

Is there a soaring eagle inside?
Is there a mountain bluebird
Waiting for spring to fly away?
Is there a meadowlark's song
Waiting to be set free?

Cedar Owen Richardson

I saw you lying there in your crib
So small—so vulnerable
Colored wires and tubes
Monitoring feeding
Supporting your life.
Tears came and
Through their prism
I could see not wires and tubes
But the miracle of love that you are.

I watched as daddy
Held you against his bare chest
For the first time.
Nothing could have been more beautiful.
The unspoken, unrehearsed
Messages you gave each other
Are printed on your hearts, never to fade.
You worked a miracle in his life that moment

Welcome into your family
Where love, shelter
And nourishing milk awaits you.
Feel the arms of love
Reaching out to embrace you.
We will never take lightly
The miracle you are.

Pain And Roses

Occasional passers by stop in admiration
The flowers respond with brilliant colors
Roses; hybrid, floribunda or heritage
Break the dullness of the cloudy day
With large blossoms and sturdy stems

Scanning the space between path and house
Their eyes are captured by lilies and
Delphiniums and clematis and begonias
Look closely friends and see
Beyond the palette to the painters soul

If you could see beneath the garden
To the gardener and the constant pain
Of muscle and sinew and weakened bones
The flowers will never reveal

You would see the soul of love
Love of flowers and life
Of children and animals
Of family and God
And a soul providing its own elixir
To heal the constant pain

All who pass by
Drink in the beauty of color
Inhale the rich fragrance
Let the balm of love so richly shared
Heal the wounds of life for you

For Rocky

Long spindly legs and tiny feet
Running walking a thousand miles
Every year of your fourteen

Friend companion guardian
Sun worshiper heat seeker
Soccer player joy bringer

Age came to you as to us all
The aches pains failing eyes and ears
Made your life so hard

You served your people well
It was time to lie down and rest
No more pain

Somewhere we do not know
A treat awaited you
Given by a loving hand

Your spirit remains
Memory may fade
Love endures

The Flame

Whenever I come away from your home
I have such a sense of well being
a smile on my face and hope in my heart
for the state of this old world

If we could bring the world
to your doorstep there would be
joy in helping others
without prejudice or selfishness
and there would be
a lot of people dancing and singing

I love your passion and
courage to pursue life
not waiting for it
to come to you whether
belly dancing or baking pizza
singing or sewing
canning or collage
there is passion in all you do.

For Adrienne at 76

Sixteen   thirty six   seventy six
add them write them erase them
still only numbers
keeping track of the tangible
that part of life we try to control
believing we can hold on to life

I celebrate your life
        not years of living
        full and beautiful
I celebrate your heart
        not years of beating
        a full and loving heart offered
I celebrate a mind
        not years of thinking
        open eager exposing truth
I celebrate a soul
        ageless loving
        open to God and neighbor
I celebrate years of sharing
the blessings of your presence

Clearing Out

Cleaning out your room of
journals and pieces of paper
on which you have written
quotes, ideas, names and
who knows what,
finding more of you here
than in the box of ashes
tucked away in the columbarium.

Your struggles with belief and faith,
your joy in family and simple things,
old greeting cards saved for years
in boxes and more boxes,
I read a few words but mostly
I just imagine how you felt
when you received that letter
from five year old Haley.

I do this now
seeking comfort
for my troubled mind.
Night time is hard
when in a troubled sleep
I hear your cries for help.

They tell me you were not in pain,
I try to believe them as I say again,
"I'm sorry," waiting to hear
a word of forgiveness.

We Dreamed Of A World

We dreamed of a world
where we were free
to love and
to be ourselves
where past was not known
where life could begin again
without expectations
where we had nothing
to be responsible for
except ourselves
few belongings
no debts
nothing to clutter our lives

I say we and yet
a doubt enters my mind
was that just my dream
I was so happy
I never asked
did I ignore
your wishes and dreams

This appears to be the end
And yet it is only the between
Of what has been written
And what is yet to come

We live our lives on that ribbon
Between miracle and mystery
Between sunrise and sunset
Between known and unknown
And embracing both we say

this is

May your life be blest in this moment—now